T0131999

Singing Sea

by Sue Maney MacVeety

El Mar que canta

Translated by Valerie Zantay

ISBN: Softcover   978-1-4134-7275-2
        Hardcover   978-1-4134-7276-9

Print information available on the last page

Rev. date: 06/17/2019

To order additional copies of this book, contact:
Xlibris
1-888-795-4274
www.Xlibris.com
Orders@Xlibris.com

Singing Sea

is dedicated to:

My Mermaid and Merman friends

Arnold Maney

Bob MacVeety

Anne Douglas

Binnie

Britha Barrett

Anne Kinne

Cecilia George

Denise George

Carol Ide

Jody Burkle

Glynis MacVeety

* and to all the people of this earth who love and respect the sea

1

"It's a secret," whispered the sea,
"Come in and swim with me."

"Tengo un secreto," susurró el mar
"Entra y nada conmigo."

3

The seafans waved to me on the shore –
"Come move with me and sway some more."

Los abanicos de mar me saludaron en la orilla - "Múevete
con nosotros, descansa más."

5

The seahorse clung to the coral so rough,
"Come dance with me 'til you've had enough."

Los caballitos de mar agarraron al aspero coral ,
"Baila con nosotros, hasta que no puedas más ."

The fish darted in schools so true
"Come watch the waves from under the blue."

Los peces lanzaron en bancos tan perfectos
"Mira las olas por debajo de su azul."

The lobster walked with its spiny shell –
"Come frolic with me, I'll never tell."

Las langostas caminaban con sus conchas tan espinosas. "Di-
viértete con nosotros, no diremos nada."

The sea serpent slithered with his mouth open wide –
He hissed, "Come let the ocean roll you with the tide."

La serpiente de mar se arrastraba con su boca abierta -
"Deja que el mar te arrastre con la marea ."

The starfish gleamed with its bright orange skin.
"Come watch with me, oh do come in."

La estrella de mar brillaba con su piel anaranjada.
"Mira conmigo, o, si entra."

The crab darted into his deep dark hole.
"Go ahead, go with them and have a roll."

El cangrejo se metio en su profundo agujero negro.
"Adelante, vete con ellos y dé una vuelta ."

The palm trees sighed with the breezes from high.

"Go ahead, be brave, give it a try."

Las palmas suspiraron con las brisas desde lo alto.

"Adelante, sé valiente, ponlo a prueba."

The mermaids sang a song so sweet.
"You must come in. You're in for a treat."

Las sirenas cantaron una cancion tan dulce.
"Deberías entrar, sera una delicia ."

The chorus continued. I couldn't stop.
I jumped right in with a splashy plop.

El coro continuó, no podía pararme.
Salté adentro con un chapoteo –! PUM!

The friendly sea and creatures within rolled me about which gave me a grin.

El mar amistoso y las criaturas adentro me arrastraron, lo cual me hizo reír.

I swam and sang until my heart filled with joy.
In the salty brine like a little buoy.

Nadé y canté hasta que mi corazón se llenó de alegría.
En el piélago salado como una pequeña boya.

The full moon rose to shine its best.

My mama called,

"Come home now child, it's time for your rest."

La luna llena subío con su brillante resplandor

Mí mamá llamó,

"Ven a casa mí hijo es hora de descansar."

"It's a secret," whispered the sea,
"come back tomorrow and swim with me."

Tengo un secreto, susurro' el mar,
"Vuelva manana y nada conmigo."

SEA EGGS

Recipe from Denise George / Grenada W.I.

Place 3 stones on the sand at the beach.

Gather sticks and place between stones.

Make a fire in between the stones. (not a strong fire)

Make coals.

Place sticks across the coals.

Rest the sea eggs (sea urchins) on the coals on top of the sticks.

When the sticks burn the eggs are ready.

Scoop eggs out with a spoon

Clean the shell and get all the spines off.

Put eggs in water.

Wash out the shells.

Season the egg with onion, garlic, and pepper and bread crumbs.

Chop these things and season it up with local stuff.

Scoop it up back into the shell.

Sprinkle bread crumbs on the top.

Put it into the oven to bake.

Serve on a bed of lettuce and tomatoes.

Very tasty and Juicy

Printed in the United States
By Bookmasters